THE WONDER OF IT ALL

THE WONDER OF IT ALL

A Daily Advent Reader
MARK SORENSEN

Copyright 2024 by Mark Sorensen

All rights reserved. No part of this publication may be reproduced, stored in a retrieval system, or transmitted, in any form or by any means—electronic, mechanical, photocopying, recording, or otherwise—without prior written permission, except for brief quotations in critical reviews or articles.

Printed in the United States of America

Scripture quotations are taken from the Holy Bible, New International Version®, NIV® Copyright ©1973, 1978, 1984, 2011 by Biblica, Inc.® Used by permission. All rights reserved worldwide.

Scripture quotations marked NRSV are taken from New Revised Standard Version Bible, copyright © 1989 National Council of the Churches of Christ in the United States of America. Used by permission. All rights reserved.

Scripture quotations marked ESV are from The Holy Bible, English Standard Version. ESV® Text Edition: 2016. Copyright © 2001 by Crossway Bibles, a publishing ministry of Good News Publishers.

Scripture quotations marked THE MESSAGE are taken THE MESSAGE. Copyright © by Eugene H. Peterson 1993, 1994, 1995, 1996, 2000, 2001, 2002. Used by permission of NavPress. All rights reserved. Represented by Tyndale House Publishers, Inc.

Cover design and layout by Nick Perreault
Page layout by PerfecType, Nashville, Tennessee

Sorensen, Mark
 The wonder of it all : a daily Advent reader / Mark Sorensen. – Franklin, Tennessee : Seedbed Publishing, ©2024.

 pages ; cm. + 1 video disc

 ISBN: 9798888000830 (paperback)
 ISBN: 9798888000861 (DVD)
 ISBN: 9798888000847 (epub)
 ISBN: 9798888000854 (updf)
 OCLC: 1438789536

 1. Advent--Meditations. 2. Advent--Prayers and devotions. 3. Devotional calendars. I. Title.

BV40.S67 2024   242/.33   2024941266

SEEDBED PUBLISHING
Franklin, Tennessee
seedbed.com

CONTENTS

Introduction: Wonder-Filled		xi
1.	Ponder This	3
2.	Kids Get It	6
3.	The Wonder in the Waiting	10
4.	I Doubt It	15
5.	A Super-Spreader Event	19
6.	Sing Out Loud, Sing Out Strong	23
7.	Origin Story	28
8.	The Wonder in the Watching	32
9.	Angel Greetings 101	37
10.	Potholes to Gardens	42
11.	Patience in the Developing	46
12.	Synchronized Heartbeats	50
13.	Stressors	54
14.	Deep Darkness and a Great Light	60
15.	The Wonder in the Searching	65

16.	Light Will Guide You Home	69
17.	Herod the (Not So) Great	73
18.	GPS: God's Positioning System	78
19.	The Wonder in the Working	83
20.	Drop the Blanket	88
21.	Big Things, Little Package	92
22.	Here's Your Sign	97
23.	Worth the Wait	101
24.	Hearers, Believers, and Preachers	106
25.	It Is God's Dark	109

There is deep within all of us a *voice*, and it speaks to us continuously, knocking on the door of our consciousness. When we are children, the voice is very loud, shattering our awareness with overwhelming clarity. Its loudness is not like a train or jet engine. It shouts to us with a whisper. . . . This voice of our childhood is the voice of wonder and amazement, the voice of God, which has always been speaking to us, even before we were born.

One sad day, we are aware of an absence. We can no longer hear the God-voice, and we are left with only silence—not a quiet silence, but a roaring silence. We did not want to stop hearing God's voice. Indeed, God kept on speaking. But our lives became louder. The increasing crescendo of our possessions, the ear-piercing noise of busyness, and the soul-smothering volume of our endless activity drowned out the still, small voice of God.

Most of us can't say *when* it happened, we only know *that* it happened. When we became aware of the absence of God's voice, there were a thousand deaths within us. Idealism and innocence died first. And across the scarred terrain of our souls, one could see the withered remains of dreams, spontaneity, poetry, passion, and ourselves—our *real* selves, the persons we were made to be.

What happened? What happened to our aliveness? How could we grow up, accumulate twelve to fifteen years of education (or more), get married, have children, work for decades, and never really live? How could we begin our lives with clarity and passion, wonder and spontaneity, yet so quickly find ourselves at the middle or end of our lives, dull and bleary-eyed, listless, and passionless?

—Mike Yaconelli, *Dangerous Wonder: The Adventure of Childlike Faith*

The world will never starve for want of wonders;
but only for want of wonder.
—G. K. Chesterton, *Tremendous Trifles*

INTRODUCTION
WONDER-FILLED

won·der
/ˈwəndər/
noun
A feeling of surprise mingled with admiration, caused by something beautiful, unexpected, unfamiliar, or inexplicable.

Let me ask you a question. When was the last time you felt *that*? Really. Take a moment and try to identify the last time that you were caught, unexpectedly, in a place of wonder.

Now, I should probably clarify. I'm not talking about the kind of wonder that seeks to answer life's great mysteries like why we drive on parkways and park on driveways. (I'm still waiting on the answer for that one, by the way.) I'm also not talking about the type of wonder where there's just a pinch of doubt mixed into whatever question you're pondering.

When I speak of wonder, I am talking about true, unbridled, uninhibited, straight-out, slack-jawed awe and wonder. Can you identify a recent moment in time when you encountered something that was so beautiful, so unexpected, so unfamiliar and incomprehensible, that it literally rendered you . . . speechless?

As I type this Advent devotional, my wife and I are babysitting our grandbaby. Simon is the first grandchild for us, and everything they say about grandparenting being the greatest thing ever, by the way, is 100-percent true. It's beyond description.

An observation about this little guy? From the moment his blue eyes came into focus, he has been all about awe and wonder. He's currently seven months old and this holiday season we've noticed that his face lights up with everything he lays his little eyes on. Literally, *everything*. Right now, he's staring at the lights on our Christmas tree while simultaneously sticking the head of a Fisher Price nativity playset character into his mouth. We're calling Simon's name, but he doesn't seem to care. Simply because he's too busy being distracted and captivated by the *wonder* of what's directly in front of him.

Perhaps it's time to rediscover the wonder found within the Advent story. What I am learning, it's not just a wonderful story, it's a wonder-*filled* story.

In the pages that follow, let's seek to rediscover the wonder found in this liturgical season of the church called Advent.

THE
WONDER
OF
IT
ALL

1
PONDER THIS

LUKE 2:19
But Mary treasured up all these things and pondered them in her heart.

CONSIDER THIS
I wish I could tell you that at an early age I was awestruck by the Christmas story. Don't get me wrong. It wasn't absent from our family tradition. In fact, from as far back as I can remember, the very first decoration that officially kicked off the holiday decor in the Sorensen family living room was our porcelain nativity set, prominently placed on top of the family piano the day after Thanksgiving. It was tradition in our house. However, it wasn't that nativity set and story that brought out my wonder; it was something completely different: the *Sears Wish Book*.

Now, I realize I may be dating myself, but back in the archaic pre-nearly-instant-delivery days of the early eighties, this little catalog was like the Holy Grail to me. As soon as it arrived in the mailbox, it never hit my parents' hands. I would carry it back to my room, sit on my bed, and slowly, page by page, take in every toy, every detail, and make meticulous notations on what I wanted to see under the tree. I was so obsessed with that catalog that one year I ripped out pages and hand-delivered them to Santa at the mall. "Hey, Santa, made it easy for you this year. Here you go! Circled, highlighted, and prioritized. Merry Christmas!"

Then came the waiting. I absolutely *loved* the anticipation of what might be sitting under that Christmas tree on December 25.

However, as I got older, the anticipation of what was under that tree on Christmas morning grew fainter and fainter. The toys lost their interest in my life and, before long, the Star Wars action figures, Legos, and Tinkertoys turned into much less exciting gifts like socks and underwear. Necessary, but no instructions needed.

And then, one year, married with my own children, we were visiting my parents and my mom pointed to a gift that was waiting for me to open under the tree. Taking the box and ripping off the paper, I was shocked to find what was waiting inside: it was the family nativity set that, as a child, we would put out together on the piano every year. What followed became our own tradition of putting out the nativity set with our own children.

I've learned to truly treasure this Advent story.

How about you?

On the other side of shepherds watching over their flock by night and angels declaring "good news of great joy . . . for all the people," Luke records that Mary "treasured up all these things" (Luke 2:8, 10, 19 ESV).

On the other side of angelic announcements, shepherds, and supposedly that cute little drummer boy who just knew the best gift to offer her was a drum solo after her delivery, Mary "pondered them in her heart."

To treasure is to store up and hold onto something of priceless value. That's the story we're stepping into together in the weeks ahead.

So, before the wondering, perhaps a fitting place to begin our Advent journey is to ponder the treasures found for us all in this nativity story of good news!

THE PRAYER

Father, we thank you for the treasure found for us all within the Christmas story. Today, open our eyes to see your presence, and our ears to hear your voice at work within our own lives and stories. In the mighty name of Jesus we pray, amen.

THE QUESTIONS

Take a look at your own nativity set that you may have or look at many of the nativity scenes you can find online or around your community. Look at each character found in the nativity scene. Who holds one of your favorite stories and why?

2
KIDS GET IT

MARK 10:13-16
People were bringing little children to Jesus for him to place his hands on them, but the disciples rebuked them. When Jesus saw this, he was indignant. He said to them, "Let the little children come to me, and do not hinder them, for the kingdom of God belongs to such as these. Truly I tell you, anyone who will not receive the kingdom of God like a little child will never enter it." And he took the children in his arms, placed his hands on them and blessed them.

CONSIDER THIS

I love the story of the mother who took her five-year-old boy with her to the small, locally owned grocery store in town. She had finished getting the groceries and went up to the counter to check out. Conveniently placed next to the register was a jar full of the most colorful pieces of hard candy you could have ever imagined.

The owner of the store who happened to be running the register that day saw the little boy staring at that jar of candies with wide-eyed wonder. Feeling a spirit of generosity, the owner asked the boy, "Would you like to reach in and grab some candy for free today?"

The boy didn't answer. He just stood there.

Pushing further, the owner replied, "Go ahead. I don't mind. Reach in! Get some candy! It's on me today."

Still, the young boy said nothing.

At a loss for what to do next, the owner asked the boy if it would be okay if *he* got some candy out for him.

With that, the little boy suddenly came alive, smiled, and said, "Please, and thank you, sir!"

The man reached in, grabbed a good-sized handful of candy, and filled the little boy's hands.

Walking out of the store, the mother was curious and asked her son, "Honey, when the nice man asked you to grab some candy out of the jar, why didn't you answer him? He asked you two different times to stick your hand in there and get some candy and you didn't move."

Without missing a beat, the boy got a huge smile on his face and replied, "Mom, did you *see* the size of his hands?"

Smart kid.

God has more wonder in his hands than we can ever realize. The question is: Are our hands ready to receive all that he has prepared to pour over us?

This brings to mind a story found in Mark's gospel, where a group of children crashed a grown-up Bible study.

Imagine the setting. Jesus was teaching, another large crowd had gathered, and the disciples were feeling like rock stars. James and John were shoulder-to-shoulder eyeing the crowd. Matthew was tediously taking notes on the teaching when, suddenly, Peter's eyes darted over to a group of kids and parents pushing through the crowd and heading straight to Jesus. *No problem*, Peter thought. *I can handle this*. Jumping into action, Peter blocked the kids and parents and quietly moved them toward the back of the crowd because, well, Jesus hadn't even gotten to the third point of that day's teaching. "Sorry, kids. Go and play somewhere else. There's serious grown-up business happening here," Peter said.

That's when it happened: Peter heard his name. I imagine that he stopped and turned around to see the crowd was now looking at *him*, caught red-handed as he was moving the kids out of the circle where the adults had gathered.

Mark records that in this moment Jesus was "indignant" (Mark 10:14a). You don't hear that word often in Scripture, by the way. In the Greek, it means to feel a violent irritation. Clearly, something is happening in the moment that we should take note of. What followed was a rebuke from Jesus: "Let the children come to me and do not hinder them, for the kingdom of God belongs to such as these." In fact, he went on to say, "anyone who will not receive the kingdom of God like a little child will never enter it" (vv. 14b–15). Then he took the children in his arms and blessed them.

Let's not miss this moment. To a group of adults, Jesus used children to show the way we're all called to enter into the presence of God. We're to enter it like a little child, hands open, ready to receive all the wonder that comes from the Father.

Today's reminder: the kingdom of God exists for kingdom children.

THE PRAYER

God of wonder, we thank you for the gift of childlike faith. It's all too easy to live our lives with clenched fists, holding on to control. Today, may we loosen the grip. May we open our hands to receive the wonder you want to freely pour over us all. In Jesus's mighty name we pray, amen.

THE QUESTIONS

What does childlike wonder mean to you?

What do children possess that adults have lost?

What does it mean to receive the kingdom of God like a little child, and where might we be missing the kingdom of God because we've grown a little too old?

3
THE WONDER IN THE WAITING

LUKE 1:5–13

In the time of Herod king of Judea there was a priest named Zechariah, who belonged to the priestly division of Abijah; his wife Elizabeth was also a descendant of Aaron. Both of them were righteous in the sight of God, observing all the Lord's commands and decrees blamelessly. But they were childless because Elizabeth was not able to conceive, and they were both very old.

Once when Zechariah's division was on duty and he was serving as priest before God, he was chosen by lot, according to the custom of the priesthood, to go into the temple of the Lord and burn incense. And when the time for the burning of incense came, all the assembled worshipers were praying outside.

Then an angel of the Lord appeared to him, standing at the right side of the altar of incense. When Zechariah saw him, he was startled and was gripped with fear. But the angel said to him: "Do not be afraid, Zechariah; your prayer has been heard. Your wife, Elizabeth, will bear you a son and you are to call him John."

CONSIDER THIS

There's a quote I love that's attributed to Mark Twain that reads: "All good things arrive unto them that wait—and don't die in the meantime."

Let's face it. Waiting can be insufferable.

Have you ever considered how much of our lives we spend waiting? A recent poll discovered that the average person spends nearly two hours a day waiting on *something*. Maybe it's waiting for someone to respond to a text, waiting for traffic to start moving again, waiting for the web page to refresh, or waiting for the latest app to download on your phone. Whatever the waiting, that time adds up. Think about it. Almost two hours a day may not sound like a lot, but eventually the numbers stack up! That's about twelve hours of waiting a week and, over the course of a year, it's more than 624 hours spent doing one laboring, excruciating task: waiting.[1]

Can I be honest? I hate waiting. Personally, waiting seems like such a waste.

What if a waiting season is not a wasted season?

Luke's Christmas story begins with Zechariah and Elizabeth. Odds are, you won't find them in your nativity set (unless you've gotten *really* creative), but theirs is

---

1. John Anderer, "Average Person Loses 26 Days Each Year to Wasted Time," Study Finds, January 17, 2022, https://studyfinds.org/loses-26-days-wasted-time/.

a love story that plays a major role in the wonder of Christ's arrival into the world.

There is a lot of Zechariah and Elizabeth's past we don't know, but in our passage today Luke gives us three very thoughtful details that are important to note: (1) They were righteous and blameless before the Lord. "Righteous" is what the Lord sees; "blameless" is what others see. One is internal, the other is external. I think it's important to note that for the children of God today it's not one or the other, it's both/and; (2) Elizabeth was barren and they were both "very old" (v. 7). How old do you have to be to be slapped with the title "very old"? We're not exactly sure. Many commentators believe they were somewhere between the ages of sixty and seventy years old. (As I write this, I am fifty-two years old. I will gladly now be referred to as a young adult!) Whatever the age was, we know this: in her waiting season, she had been unable to conceive and give Zechariah a child; and (3) Luke reminds us that Zechariah was of the priestly division of Abijah and about to serve out his priestly duties in the temple.

That's the context.

For Zechariah, it was an ordinary day. But on this ordinary day, God had an extraordinary revelation waiting just around the corner.

As lots were cast, Zechariah's name came up and he was given the incredible opportunity to go into the temple of the Lord and burn incense. It's believed that as many as 18,000 to 20,000 priests gathered in Jerusalem to serve various positions in the temple during a two-week period. Many served their entire lives and never got the chance that Zechariah got to enter the temple and burn incense before the Lord.

What a moment! I can imagine Zechariah's heart skipped a few beats when he saw his name drawn. However, little did Zechariah know that his heart was about to get a serious workout as, just beyond the door of the temple, an angelic encounter awaited.

As Zechariah's eyes fell on Gabriel, he heard the following words declared over him: "Do not be afraid, Zechariah; your prayer has been heard. Your wife Elizabeth will bear you a son, and you are to call him John" (v. 13).

I wonder: How long had Zechariah been praying for he and Elizabeth to have a child? Forty years? Thirty years? Twenty? Honestly, was it even a prayer within the past ten years? Had he given up completely on the hope of ever having a child? We don't know. But we know this, it was a prayer he *had* prayed. In that moment, Gabriel declared five little words that, if we're not careful, we might completely miss in the story: *your prayer has been heard*.

Two reminders for today: (1) You may see this as an ordinary day. Look out—God may have extraordinary moments waiting for you around the corner, and (2) the Lord hears your prayers, my friend. He knows your heart, and he loves the sound of your voice.

THE PRAYER

Loving God, we thank you that, even in a waiting season, it's not a wasted season. Today, open our eyes to the truth found in your Word that our prayers are heard and, even greater, allow that truth to travel from our head to hearts.

THE QUESTIONS

How are you in the waiting?

In what areas in your life are you "waiting upon the Lord"?

What might the Lord be saying to you in this season?

4
I DOUBT IT

LUKE 1:18–20
Zechariah asked the angel, "How can I be sure of this? I am an old man and my wife is well along in years."

The angel said to him, "I am Gabriel. I stand in the presence of God, and I have been sent to speak to you and to tell you this good news. And now you will be silent and not able to speak until the day this happens, because you did not believe my words, which will come true at their appointed time."

CONSIDER THIS
Okay, let's talk "doubt" for a moment. But before we do, I must give credit to Zechariah. He gets major brownie points in his response to Gabriel. When he learned the news that Elizabeth was going to have a baby, he brought up the fact that he's old, and then, when faced with saying the same of his wife, he slowed down and carefully used the phrase that she's "well along in years."

Well played, Zechariah. Well played.

Yet something he said struck a serious chord with the angel Gabriel and it wasn't Zechariah's old-age comment. It was the words he used *before* stating the obvious: *"How can I be sure of this?"*

That, my friends, is the scent of doubt overpowering the incense of the wonder found in that moment.

How many times does our doubt literally get in the way of the wonder that God has placed in our paths?

As I write this, our doorbell just rang, and a courier left a package on our front doorstep. Apparently, my wife has ordered some baby gates that we need to put up in our home. With the gift of a grandchild in our lives comes the added bonus of making sure the house is grandbaby-proofed. It's never a bad idea to put up some boundaries to keep our sweet little ones from crawling into places that may be unsafe.

Baby gates are handy, but let's be real, they're not meant to be permanently installed. Children grow into teenagers who grow into adults, and whether we want it or not, the world becomes one big, open, and, oftentimes, scary place.

Here's the problem with growing older. If we're not careful, we run the risk of putting baby gates back up in our paths, closing ourselves off from the hopes, dreams, and plans the Lord may still have for us! Perhaps it's just safer to wall up those God-given wants rather than lean in and continue to intercede for our heart's desires.

Zechariah, a devout follower of the Lord who both knew the words and promises of God and who had literally just won the lottery moments earlier and was now standing in the temple, had just heard the miraculous. With the angel Gabriel in his midst, he has learned that the Messiah was coming into the world as told by the prophet Micah four hundred years earlier, and Zechariah's own son would be the very one, "in the spirit . . . of Elijah, to . . . make ready a people prepared for the Lord" (v. 17).

I love Gabriel's response to Zechariah's doubt. He simply replies: "I am Gabriel. I stand in the presence of God, and I have been sent to speak to you and to tell you this good news. And now, you will be silent and not able to speak until the day this happens, because you did not believe my words, which will come true at their appointed time."

Zechariah had closed the door on a dream, and when the path was revealed, he couldn't see the wonder that was staring at him within the moment. Gabriel's response, in effect: "Why don't we just zip up that mouth of yours so, moving forward, your words don't overshadow the wonder God is prophesying over you in this moment?"

Perhaps Zechariah's faith had weakened over time. If we're going to be honest, it happens to us all too. Yet here's the good news found in today's word: weak faith does not weaken God's power.

THE PRAYER

God of wonder, we thank you for the reminder that where there is breath in our lungs, there's a story that's still being written. Awaken our hearts and open our hands to receive the words of hope you would breathe over us today.

THE QUESTIONS

Where are our words getting in the way of the wonder God might be speaking over us today?

Where have we put baby gates back up in our stories that God might be wanting us to remove?

5
A SUPER-SPREADER EVENT

LUKE 1:65–66
All the neighbors were filled with awe, and throughout the hill country of Judea people were talking about all these things. Everyone who heard this wondered about it, asking, "What then is this child going to be?" For the Lord's hand was with him.

CONSIDER THIS

Zechariah was served a sentence of silence from Gabriel. Not a life sentence, mind you, just a period of nine months. It's worthy to note the following: nine months equals thirty-nine weeks, which is a grand total of 273 days. That's a culmination of 6,552 hours of no speaking, no talking, no chance of letting his vocalized doubts get in the way of the wonder of the dream that God was birthing in Elizabeth in that moment.

So Zechariah emerged from the temple speechless.

Don't forget, Zechariah had entered the temple to burn some incense. It's not a long process. But, as the time passed, I am guessing the other priests started looking at their watches and suspecting *something* was happening. When Zechariah emerged, he emerged without words. The other priests had to know something was up, but Zechariah couldn't tell them about it.

He made it back to Elizabeth and, through pen and paper, shared with her the good news of what was being done, to which she sweetly replied, "The Lord has done this for me" (Luke 1:25).

The months passed and the day came that Elizabeth would give birth to a son. Luke records what happened next:

> On the eighth day they came to circumcise the child, and they were going to name him after his father Zechariah, but his mother spoke up and said, "No! He is to be called John."
>
> They said to her, "There is no one among your relatives who has that name."
>
> Then they made signs to his father, to find out what he would like to name the child. He asked for a writing tablet, and to everyone's astonishment he wrote, "His name is John." Immediately, his mouth was opened and his tongue set free, and he began to speak, praising God. (1:59–64)

As incredible as this whole story is, it's the verse that follows that I want to highlight.

Luke says that, as the neighbors *watched* all of this play out, they were "*filled* with awe, and throughout the hill country of Judea people were *talking* about all these things" (v. 65, emphasis mine). Do you see the progression? As people saw the miracles of God play out, they watched, they were filled, and they told others about what they had seen.

Here's what I love about wonder: *wonder is contagious.*

Think about this. We have the gospel today because of the wonder that has been passed down through the generations telling the stories of the movement of God among his people. In fact, go back to the very beginning of the church in Acts 2. You find that the early believers "devoted themselves to the apostles' teaching and to fellowship, to the breaking of bread and to prayer" (v. 42). What followed? "Everyone was filled with awe at the many wonders and signs performed by the apostles" (v. 43). What happened next was this: "And the Lord added to their number daily those who were being saved" (v. 47b).

Who is watching *us* today? What stories of wonder are we proclaiming, and what are people saying about the work of God in and among us? The psalmist says, "Give thanks to the Lord, for he is good; his love endures forever. Let the redeemed of the Lord tell their story—those he redeemed from the hand of the foe" (Ps. 107:1–2).

Our good news for today is this: the gospel and our story is not just a gift to be treasured; it is a gift to be shared.

THE PRAYER

Gracious God, we thank you for the good news that is found in the Advent story. In a world where the news channels don't often lead with good news, we, as your children, get to declare it all through our lives. Today, may we intentionally lean in to both the wonder found in this story and the wonder that needs to be shared with those you place in our paths. Amen.

THE QUESTIONS

Can you think of a time when someone shared a story of God's wonder and work in their lives with you?

What is a story of God's work in your life that you could share as an encouragement to someone else today?

6
SING OUT LOUD, SING OUT STRONG

LUKE 1:67–79
His father Zechariah was filled with the Holy Spirit and prophesied:

"Praise be to the Lord, the God of Israel,
  because he has come to his people and redeemed them.
He has raised up a horn of salvation for us
  in the house of his servant David
(as he said through his holy prophets of long ago),
salvation from our enemies
  and from the hand of all who hate us—
to show mercy to our ancestors
  and to remember his holy covenant,
  the oath he swore to our father Abraham:
to rescue us from the hand of our enemies,
  and to enable us to serve him without fear
  in holiness and righteousness before him all our days.

And you, my child, will be called a prophet of the Most High;
  for you will go on before the Lord to prepare the way
    for him,
to give his people the knowledge of salvation

through the forgiveness of their sins,
because of the tender mercy of our God,
   by which the rising sun will come to us from heaven
to shine on those living in darkness
   and in the shadow of death,
to guide our feet into the path of peace."

CONSIDER THIS

I have always loved singing. In fact, I'm pretty sure I can recall the first song I remember singing to family and friends, thanks to my avid watching of the children's television show *Sesame Street*. The song was simply called "Sing." The Carpenters would record it in 1973, and it would go on to be a hit on the Billboard charts. I loved this happy song.

Song and singing runs throughout my family tree. Perhaps that's why one of my favorite scenes from a holiday film centers around the beauty and importance of song found in the holiday classic *Elf*. No one really grabs ahold of childlike Christmastime wonder quite like Buddy the Elf.

If you've seen the movie, no doubt you recall the scene.

On this particular day, Buddy wanders into the toy department at Gimbels store. He's talking to his friend and coworker Jovie, who's not in the best of moods, and Buddy makes a simple observation: "Sounds like someone needs to sing a Christmas carol." To say that

Jovie's not receptive to the idea is an understatement as, according to her, she doesn't sing. However, Buddy is relentless and won't give up. And that's when Jovie confesses, "I *can* sing, I just choose *not* to sing. Especially in front of other people." Buddy can't accept her lack of holiday cheer and shows her how it's done.

Before Zechariah's encounter with the angel Gabriel, I'm not sure if Zechariah was pro singing in public or anti singing in public. However, after his voice returned, we learn something about him that we all could take a few pointers from: on the other side of the wonder in the waiting, there was a song of wonder just waiting to be heard.

Did you know that there are four Advent songs attributed to Luke's Christmas story?

- Mary's song (1:46–55)
- The angels' song (2:13–14)
- Simeon's song (2:28–32)
- Zechariah's song (1:67–79)

Think about this song of Zechariah. Four hundred years of silence stood between a word of hope that the last prophet in the Old Testament, Malachi, received and this word of salvation and the coming Messiah spoken by Gabriel in Luke 1. Add to those four hundred years an additional nine months from Gabriel's revelation to Zechariah and his doubt until little John came into the world. Once his voice returned, Zechariah was ready to sing of all the Lord had done and of his wonders and grace. It didn't matter if his singing voice was pleasant or not; Zechariah didn't care. He just needed to sing!

He sang with a heart looking back on the story of God's people, the story of the redemption and salvation found in God's promises which are everlasting. He sang of the promise of deliverance from our enemies, the mercy and grace extended to our ancestors, and the freedom to worship him without fear, in holiness and righteousness, as long as we live.

So what about you? Is there a song in your heart that needs to be sung today? Go ahead. Take a few pointers from Zechariah. Look back and remember where God has met you in your story. Then look forward! Remember God's promises and trust in his provision. Then sing!

THE PRAYER

God of wonder, our prayer is the words found in Lamentations 3:22–23: "Because of the LORD's great love, we are not consumed, for his compassions never fail. They are new every morning; great is your faithfulness." We rejoice in your great love. May that be the song we sing today with our very lives. Amen.

THE QUESTIONS

How do you feel about singing?

Is there a song in your heart today that you could sing? What would that look like for you? What would that song be?

7
ORIGIN STORY

GENESIS 3:15
*"And I will put enmity
 between you and the woman,
 and between your offspring and hers;
he will crush your head,
 and you will strike his heel."*

CONSIDER THIS

I love a good origin story. Maybe that's why I have always been a sucker for comic books and superhero movies. Whether it's how Tony Stark became Iron Man, how Bruce Banner became the (not-so-jolly) green giant, or how Bruce Wayne became so obsessed with bats that he started to dress like one, the joy for me in their stories—or any good origin story, for that matter—is this: discovering where and how it all began.

With that in mind, did you know the Christmas story has an origin story? Spoiler alert: it didn't begin in the manger; it began in a garden.

Today, let's go back to the beginning.

In Genesis 1 and 2, you find not only the creation story but also the origin story of humanity. The Word says it was from the dust that "the Lord God formed a man" and "breathed into his nostrils the breath of life" (2:7). Translation: Adam took his first breath in the garden. What follows is this, the Lord declared: "It is not good for the man to be alone" (v. 18a). So, with the help of a really good Holy Spirit–infused nap and Adam's rib, God added to the population of Eden by one and Eve entered into the story.

Now, this is important. Don't miss this. God's intent for his creation was twofold: Adam and Eve dwelled in relationship with one another, as well as in relationship with their heavenly Father. As chapter 2 ends, we see the following words: "they felt no shame" (v. 25).

Shame was never intended to be a part of the origin story of creation. How beautiful . . .

Oh, how I wish the story ended there. Sorry to say, it doesn't.

There's a Genesis 3.

It is here where the Tempter slithered into the garden and that which was forbidden became enticing. With that first forbidden taste, something that never belonged in God's origin story with humanity stepped in: shame.

Actions have consequences. As a result of eating the forbidden fruit, the Lord had some words for Adam and Eve. There were certainly repercussions for their choosing the Serpent's voice over God's, but the Lord had some words for the Serpent as well. There was a curse and a promise: "I will put enmity between you and the woman, and between your offspring and hers; he will crush your head, and you will strike his heel" (3:15).

In a sense, it's here that God said to the Serpent, "You don't get to rewrite the story of redemption for my creation." In what was arguably one of the worst moments in all the Bible where sin entered the story, we're reminded that God had a plan. It was the promise of a Savior who would correct what Adam and Eve could not do and restore us back into right relationship with the Father. I've heard it said that Genesis 3:15 is the first gospel of the Old Testament. It's a New Testament promise in an Old Testament story.

Today, let the origin story from the manger take us back to the garden. Shame may have stepped into the story of humanity, but the arrival of Jesus into the world was the fulfillment of God's promise and the coming victory over the Enemy. That's good news for us all.

THE PRAYER

Heavenly Father, we thank you for your unwavering and relentless love that has pursued us from the very beginning. May we remember that what began in the garden was birthed in a manger, nailed to a cross, and walked out of a tomb—and it is but one story of your never-ending love that pursues us all today. Amen.

THE QUESTIONS

What does this origin story mean to you? Where do you see yourself inside God's origin story today?

8
THE WONDER IN THE WATCHING

LUKE 1:26–28
In the sixth month of Elizabeth's pregnancy, God sent the angel Gabriel to Nazareth, a town in Galilee, to a virgin pledged to be married to a man named Joseph, a descendent of David. The virgin's name was Mary. The angel went to her and said, "Greetings, you who are highly favored! The Lord is with you."

CONSIDER THIS

In his book *The Fiddler in the Subway*, Gene Weingarten tells the story of Joshua Bell, a world-famous violinist, who donned a baseball cap, grabbed his $3.5-million-dollar Stradivarius violin, and stood on a platform in a crowded Washington, DC, subway station to test a theory. Bell was accustomed to playing for sold-out venues around the world but, on this day, for forty-three minutes, he played his violin amid the busy commuters walking by to see who would notice. It's recorded that 1,097 people passed by and he earned a measly thirty-two dollars in change and tips.

Here's the fun part. Out of the nearly 1,100 people who walked by him, one person, a young lady named Stacy, was the only one to recognize the world-renowned violinist. When she recognized Bell, she stood ten feet away with a huge smile plastered on her face. She was astonished at the fact that here was a world-class violinist playing, and people were casually passing by, tossing quarters at a man who gets paid professionally to sold-out concert halls. Her response: "What kind of a city do I live in that this could happen?"[2]

Poet Elizabeth Barrett Browning made the following observation:

> . . . Earth's crammed with heaven,
> And every common bush afire with God:
> But only he who sees, takes off his shoes;
> The rest sit round it, and pluck blackberries . . .[3]

I think about this quote often in relationship to the Christmas story. If the people in our nativity sets

---

2. Gene Weingarten, *The Fiddler in the Subway: The True Story of What Happened When a World-Class Violinist Played for Handouts . . . and Other Virtuoso Performances by America's Foremost Feature Writer* (New York: Simon & Schuster, 2010), 360.

3. Elizabeth Barrett Browning, *Aurora Leigh* (1857; repr., Oxford University Press, 2008), 246.

are wearing shoes, the truth is, none of them should have been—because holy ground was breaking out all around them.

In Luke's gospel, sandwiched between Zechariah's angelic encounter and his nine months of silence, we find the angel Gabriel making another stop on his Advent journey to someone else we are going to spend a little time with. Her name: Mary.

I'd love to know the context of exactly *what* Mary was doing when Gabriel arrived on the scene. We don't really know those details. We only know where Mary *was*; she was in Nazareth, a small town with a population of less than two hundred people. It was here that Gabriel arrived onto the platform of Mary's story.

In the days that follow, let's take some time to dig into the wonder found in Mary's angelic encounter. For today, let's just pause and sit with the eleven words Gabriel spoke over the soon-to-be mother of Jesus: "Greetings, you who are highly favored! The Lord is with you."

I love this word that Gabriel used with Mary: *favored.*

To be favored means to be *both endowed and enriched* in God's grace. What follows favor? After Gabriel spoke of God's favor and grace that was *on* Mary, he said, "The Lord is with you." What a statement! What Gabriel was saying is this: "Mary, not only is God's grace *with* you, but God's grace is also at work around you!"

This Advent story is a reminder: "For God so loved the world that he gave his one and only Son, that whoever believes in him shall not perish but have eternal life" (John 3:16). That is favor, my friends. Let's not stop there, however. John's gospel goes on to say, "For God did not send his Son into the world to condemn the world, but to save the world through him" (v. 17). This is the beauty of grace.

Perhaps today is a good day to stop and get lost in the wonder of this truth.

Let's find a moment to remove our shoes and remember that the places we are standing are holy indeed, for the Lord is near. Let's look up from our calendars and schedules in the rush of the season to listen to the music of favor and grace that the God of the universe is playing over us and around us all.

No matter the circumstances, the words to Mary meet us within the context of Jesus today: "Greetings, you who are highly favored! The Lord is with you."

That is good news for us all.

THE PRAYER

God of wonder, we pause today to remember that not only is your favor on us because of the love found in Jesus, but your presence is also with us. Today, we thank you for favor and presence. In Jesus's name, amen.

THE QUESTIONS

What does favor mean to you? How does this story change your definition?

How can you lift your eyes today and see the greater story God is playing in and around you?

9
ANGEL GREETINGS 101

LUKE 1:29–34

Mary was greatly troubled at his words and wondered what kind of greeting this might be. But the angel said to her, "Do not be afraid, Mary; you have found favor with God. You will conceive and give birth to a son, and you are to call him Jesus. He will be great and will be called the Son of the Most High. The Lord God will give him the throne of his father David, and he will reign over Jacob's descendants forever; his kingdom will never end."

"How will this be," Mary asked the angel, "since I am a virgin?"

CONSIDER THIS

Before an angel gets sent to earth to give us humans divine words, messages, or instructions, I wonder if they have to attend angel training first. In my mind, I can almost see it. Imagine an ornate angelic classroom where Gabriel calmly walks to the front of the room; clears his throat, calling the class to attention; and says the following:

"Okay, class! If I can have your attention. Settle down. Find your seats, please. Today's class is on the subject of 'How to speak with humans and not scare them to death.' This is a short lesson but an instrumental one. Really, it's all about how you open the conversation. There are four words you will want you memorize, rehearse, and remember, as they are key in any interaction you have with a human being." Seeing this as a teaching moment, Gabriel asks, "Any guesses as to what those words might be?"

Silence falls on the room. One angel on the front row timidly raises his hands and replies, "*Please don't run away?*"

"Good answer; however, nope. Not right," Gabriel replies.

A few moments pass and another angel's hand goes up. "*Hey, neighbor, got a minute?*"

Gabriel shakes his head and replies, "That's five words and, nope, still not right."

After more silence, Gabriel, walks to the chalkboard and writes the following four words down in all caps, instructing all the angels to copy them down and remember them. The words on the board are as follows:
DO NOT BE AFRAID.

Class dismissed.

Have you noticed that, when you read the interactions between angels and humans, "Do not be afraid" seems to always be the token opening statement? Angelic encounters can be terrifying. When you read the descriptions of angels in Isaiah or Revelation, I think "do not be afraid" is the perfect way for an angel to start.

However, it's interesting that when Gabriel met with Mary, he used a different script. He didn't open with the phrase, "Do not be afraid." Instead, it was, "Greetings, you who are highly favored! The Lord is with you" (Luke 1:28). On the other side of that, what do you find? "Mary was . . . troubled . . . and wondered what kind of greeting this might be" (v. 29).

Having learned that she's favored and that the Lord is with her, Mary's next thought is not one of fear because a literal angel is standing before her. Instead, her opening thought: *I'm favored by the Lord? Uh-oh. That can't be good.*

Now, pay attention to what happened next. Gabriel, once again, repeated that she's favored, and then delivered the news that the Messiah will come through her womb. Notice what follows. She didn't *doubt*; instead, she *wondered*. It's interesting that this was a very different reaction than that of Zechariah. Remember, when Zechariah heard his news, he replies, "How can I *know* that this will happen? For I am an old man, and my wife is getting on in years" (1:18 NRSV, emphasis mine). Yet here Mary simply asked, "How will this *be*, since I am a virgin?" (emphasis mine).

Remember, she was betrothed to Joseph. To be betrothed was very much like a marriage, minus the consummation. However, when she learned that a child would come through her womb—and not just any child, the promised Messiah, God in flesh—the only question Mary asked was not one of doubt, but one of wonder. *Where Zechariah saw obstacles, Mary saw the miracle and wondered at how it would play out.*

Did you know that most commentators and scholars believe Mary was anywhere between twelve and fourteen years of age? For all intents and purposes, she was still a child, and I wonder if perhaps that's where the childlike wonder she possessed in this moment came from—her own youth.

Mary, in this quiet and beautiful moment, didn't understand the "how." Not by any stretch of the imagination. Yet, she did understand the *who* that was behind it.

The thought for today: we don't always get the full picture when it comes to God's plan and workings in our life. It's difficult to know how God will carry us through. Yet let childlike wonder take over in those moments and say to yourself the following: "I may not know the how, but thank you, Jesus, I know the who. 'I AM' will always be enough for me."

THE PRAYER

Eternal God, you hold everything in perfect balance in the palm of your hands. That includes me. Give me the peace to trust and the patience to walk with you and not run ahead of you. In Jesus's name, amen.

THE QUESTIONS

What encourages you through Mary's reaction and response to Gabriel? What challenges you?

What would it look like for you to move from doubt to wonder in your own life?

10
POTHOLES TO GARDENS

LUKE 1:35–37
The angel answered, "The Holy Spirit will come on you, and the power of the Most High will overshadow you. So the holy one to be born will be called the Son of God. Even Elizabeth your relative is going to have a child in her old age, and she who was said to be unable to conceive is in her sixth month. For no word from God will ever fail."

CONSIDER THIS

I read a news story recently about a pothole that was plaguing a small neighborhood town in Toronto, Canada. The neighborhood had done everything they could think of to get the city to fix the pothole. After petitioning the city and getting signatures to have it corrected, the city finally went to work and filled the hole. However, what they had hoped would correct the problem didn't last. It came back. In fact, it was even larger the second time around. Needless to say, the neighborhood was furious about it and had no idea what to do or how this was going to get fixed. That is, until the day something completely unexpected happened.

As motorists drove by, they saw weeds growing out of the pothole. Only, it wasn't weeds. Upon closer inspection, it was a tomato plant. Not just one, mind you; there were several of them. The best part is they were growing out of the middle of that annoying pothole. So what happened? Someone, under the cover of night, snuck into the middle of the road and filled the pothole with loads of potting soil and then proceeded to plant all the tomato plants inside it.

What do you do now with a pothole growing tomato plants in the middle of a busy street? You make a community garden out of it, that's what you do! The city was caught off guard as the residents roped off the pothole and claimed it as their own personal tomato garden.

I wonder if the pothole-sized places of doubt, uncertainty, and questions found in our faith story might actually hold something beautiful inside of it, provided we trust God long enough to cultivate the soil and grow beauty within it.

Our scripture today takes us a little deeper into the wonder that Mary carried with her after Gabriel's announcement about the coming birth of Christ.

On the other side of Mary's wonder as to the *how* regarding the immaculate conception, Gabriel spoke to the *who*. He simply replied: "The Holy Spirit will come on you, and the power of the Most High will overshadow you" (Luke 1:35a).

Gabriel used the word *overshadow* here. Did you know that's the same word used in relationship to the transfiguration moment found in the Gospels where Peter, James, and John went with Jesus up the mountain and, all of a sudden, the presence of God overshadowed them (Matt. 17:1–8; Mark 9:2–8; Luke 9:28–36 ESV)? Imagine, God's holiness appeared in a cloud, and it was so thick that they found themselves in the presence of God. When they looked behind them, there was God. When they looked to the right, God; to the left, God. Literally, wherever they looked, there was God. Now here Gabriel used the *same* word. In a sense, Gabriel was saying, "Mary, I know you're scared, but listen, in this uncertain season the presence of the Most High is with you. And not just with you, the presence of the Most High is overshadowing you! So much so, that you will never have to question where God is. He will be seen all over your story."

How did Gabriel end this message to Mary? "For no word from God will ever fail" (Luke 1:37). The English Standard Version says it this way: "For nothing will be impossible with God."

Today, I feel the Spirit calling us to linger with the word *overshadowed*.

It's easy to focus on the pothole. But what if God is growing something right in the middle of the mess?

To know this Christmas story is to know our story. We're loved. We're valued. We're overshadowed by the promises and presence of God. Here is the best part: "For nothing will be impossible with God."

Let that truth take root in the middle of whatever pothole you're looking at, and see what God can grow as a result.

THE PRAYER

Loving Father, nothing is impossible to you. Where we see limitations and impossibilities, you see so much more than we could ever imagine. Holy Spirit, give us strength, courage, and open eyes to see your overwhelming and overshadowing presence in and among us. In Jesus's name, amen.

THE QUESTIONS

What is the Spirit saying to you within this story today? Can you identify the potholes in your own story?

Could God be growing beauty in brokenness?

Where do you see God overshadowing you in your story?

11
PATIENCE IN THE DEVELOPING

LUKE 1:38
"I am the Lord's servant," Mary answered. "May your word to me be fulfilled." Then the angel left her.

CONSIDER THIS
My wife and I recently came across a box in our attic that had been taped up for quite some time. In it, we made a rather surprising and dated discovery. We found several tubes containing undeveloped 35mm film canisters.[4] Now *there* is a memory. Does anyone else remember taking pictures with your Kodak cameras? There was nothing quite like the elation of clicking that last photo, only to hear the whir of the 35mm film advancing to the end. Next was the thrill of popping the canister out, taking it to the local drug store or pharmacy, and waiting five to seven days to get the pictures developed and returned—only to find that your thumb

---

4. For those reading this that may have no clue what I am talking about, I will pause while you Google that. Go ahead. Look it up.

was over the lens and half the pictures were unusable. At least, that was my experience.

Of course, today it's a completely different world. We no longer need a camera because a vast majority of us have one on our phones. We simply see the moment, take a picture with our phone, and it's ready for immediate viewing. There is no more waiting. And the added bonus if you don't like it, delete it and try again. Is the coloring off? No worries, you can instantly fix that as well. Look, there are certainly advantages to our technology today. There is no denying that. Yet I also can't help but wonder if we've become addicted to the "instant viewing." Maybe, just maybe, we have lost the wonder found in the "yet to be developed."

When it comes to getting the full picture of what God might be doing in our lives, we all want the God of Instant Delivery. Make the request, and it's delivered same-day service on the doorsteps of our heart. What I have found is that God rarely works that quickly. Perhaps there's great beauty to be found in the waiting and watching the picture that God is developing in our stories over time.

The older I get, the more I am starting to see that my faith story is more like that 35 MM film canister than a digital photo. When seasons of doubt, insecurity, and anxiety take place, I have to pause and remember that what I may not see now, in time God will develop that picture for me. The more I wait in patience, little by little, it comes into view. The secret is this: trust him and be patient in the waiting.

Having heard the incredible news that she was favored, that no word from God would ever fail, that the Holy Spirit would come upon her, and through her womb the Messiah would come, Mary simply responded with the following: "I am the Lord's servant. May your word to me be fulfilled." I never cease to be challenged by Mary's trusting, steadfast, and childlike faith.

Bible commentator William Barclay said this of her response: "Mary's submission is a very lovely thing. 'Whatever God says, I accept.' Mary had learned to forget the world's commonest prayer—'Thy will be *changed*'—and to pray the world's greatest prayer—'Thy will be *done*.'"[5]

Today, rest in the waiting.

THE PRAYER

God of wonder, we pray in the Lord's Prayer these words, "Give us this day our daily bread."[6] Meaning, we trust that today you are giving us exactly what we need—no

---

5. William Barclay, "Commentary on Luke 1," *William Barclay's Daily Study Bible*, https://www.studylight.org/commentaries/eng/dsb/luke-1.html. Emphasis added.
6. Matthew 6:11 (ESV).

more, no less. Help us to be content in today because you are already meeting our needs tomorrow. Amen.

THE QUESTIONS

What are the areas of your life still in development? Where is God saying to you, "be patient" in the waiting?

12
SYNCHRONIZED HEARTBEATS

LUKE 1:46b–48
*"My soul glorifies the Lord
 and my spirit rejoices in God my Savior,
for he has been mindful
 of the humble state of his servant.
From now on all generations will call me blessed[.]"*

CONSIDER THIS

Before I ever stepped into ministry as a profession, I was a disc jockey at a radio station in the little East Texas town I grew up in. For almost ten years, I spun records and played the best of the '50s, '60s, and early '70s. I loved being a DJ. In fact, one of my favorite segments called "Did You Know?" was one I would do every Friday morning. Each week, I would scour the various news wires and magazines in search of interesting statistics, world records, scientific facts, and random pieces of trivia, and carry that as a news segment for listeners.

It's funny the things that have spilled over from my radio life into my preaching life. I have been out of radio for more than twenty-five years now, but to this day, I still save stories that interest me. In a preacher's world, "Sunday is always coming," and a good sermon illustration is always handy to have on hand. So, when I read Mary's famous song known as the Magnificat (Luke 1:46b–55), I can't help but recall a study that I came across in my reading.

Curious researchers at a university in Gothenburg, Sweden, wanted to know what happened to the heart rates of high school choir members when they joined their voices and sang together in song. Using pulse monitors attached to the members' ears, the researchers monitored changes found in their heartbeats as they navigated through a choral piece of music, and what they found surprised them. In a very short period of time, the different singers in the choir didn't just unify their voices, "their pulse rates also synchronized, their hearts beating together in relationship to their breaths."[7] How cool is that? Quite literally, not only were they singing together and alongside one another, their own hearts were beating in unison as well.

---

7. Megan McGrath, "Choirs Synchronize Heartbeats Along with Voices," VOA, July 10, 2013, https://www.voanews.com/a/choirs-synchronize-heartbeats-along-with-voices/1699072.html.

I truly believe that there is something beautiful that happens when we sing together. Even more beautiful is when our hearts are in sync with God's heart.

In Mary's song, I like to think that this was the case as she sang before the Lord. Not only was she singing with her voice, but I wonder if her heartbeat synched in perfect rhythm to the very one inside her womb, Jesus, Immanuel, God with us.

Today, let's look at the first few verses of Mary's song to the Lord.

Mary sang, "My soul magnifies the Lord" (v. 46b ESV). To magnify something doesn't make the object bigger, it simply helps us see the object for what it truly is. How easy would it have been for Mary to magnify the fear, uncertainty, or all the questions that stood ahead of her, but she didn't. She chose to magnify the Lord for who he is and what he was doing in her midst. Mary magnified the Lord. But she didn't stop there.

She also rejoiced. Mary sang, "my spirit rejoices in God my Savior" (v. 47). Here in this moment, her joy was not rooted in her status or position, but in God, her heavenly Father. Joy based on circumstances, status, or position can easily fluctuate and change. Joy that is rooted in the unchanging love of God is a joy that withstands.

From there, she declared the following: "for he has been mindful of the humble state of his servant" (v. 48a).

The beauty in this stanza is found here. Mary had an exalted view of God, not in herself. That is humility. God can *and* will always work with hearts that are humble. God specializes in using ordinary people whose limitations make them ideal showcases for his greatness and glory.

Mary magnified, she rejoiced, and she showed incredible humility.

That's a song we all can join in on.

THE PRAYER

Eternal God, today we magnify your name and rejoice in your abundant love and provision found within our lives. May your presence fill our hearts with joy and guide us in all we say and do. In Jesus's name, amen.

THE QUESTIONS

Mary magnified, rejoiced, and recognized the greatness of God in comparison to who and whose she was. Where does this encourage you, and how does this challenge you today?

13
STRESSORS

LUKE 1:49–50

*"[F]or the Mighty One has done great things for me—
    holy is his name.
His mercy extends to those who fear him,
    from generation to generation."*

CONSIDER THIS

Let's talk about stressors for just a moment.

Have you ever heard about the Holmes-Rahe Stress Scale?[8] It was developed in 1967 by two psychiatrists, Thomas Holmes and Richard Rahe, who examined the medical records of more than five thousand medical patients to determine whether stressful events might cause illnesses in their lives. What resulted in this study was a list of forty-three life events, each given a number that, when added up, if higher than 300, serves as a warning that you're at a dangerously high-risk level for illness.

---

8. Arlin Cuncic, "What Is the Holmes and Rahe Stress Scale?" Verywell Mind, November 17, 2022, https://www.verywellmind.com/what-is-the-holmes-and-rahe-stress-scale-6455916.

There is no doubt that the holidays certainly bring with it a fair amount of stress, but have you ever considered what that first Christmas season was like for Mary and Joseph? Well, let's put their story to the Holmes-Rahe stress test, shall we?

Within the context of those days leading up to that first Christmas morning, Mary and Joseph were dealing with matters of a pending marriage (50 points), a possible marriage separation (65 points), marital reconciliation (45 points), pregnancy (40 points), adding new family members (39 points), changes in their financial state (38 points), trouble with in-laws (29 points), change in living conditions (25 points), a change in working conditions (20 points), and changes in residence (20 points). The list goes on—that's just to name a few.[9]

Adding all the stressors as noted in the Holmes-Rahe stress test, they would have scored more than *400 points*! Remember, the marker for the danger level is 300. I think it's safe to say they were *quite* stressed in the middle of that first Christmas story!

Look at how Mary responded to all that was uncertain, beyond her control, and beyond her ability

---

9. "Mary and Joseph on Holmes Rahe Stress Scale," Preaching Today, https://www.preachingtoday.com/illustrations/2015/december/3120715.html.

to correct the variables. She simply sang out the following words: "for the Mighty One has done great things for me—holy is his name. His mercy extends to those who fear him, from generation to generation" (Luke 1:49–50).

Amid the stress and weakness found in the uncertainty, Mary proclaimed three beautiful truths.

First, she remembered that "the Mighty One has done great things for me" (v. 49a). It's clear because of Mary's faith that she knew the Scriptures. I wonder, as Mary sang, did the songs found in the Psalms came to mind? Perhaps Psalm 89?

The psalmist declares:

> I will sing of the Lord's great love forever;
>> with my mouth I will make your faithfulness known
>
>> through all generations.
>
> I will declare that your love stands firm forever,
>> that you have established your faithfulness in heaven itself. . . .
>
> Who is like you, Lord God Almighty?
>> You, Lord, are mighty, and your faithfulness surrounds you." (1–2, 8)

I saw a bumper sticker once that said, "Jesus saves us from all that plagues us." Not a bad reminder, honestly.

Trust your weakness to a mighty God, and stand on that solid foundation.

Next, Mary focused on the holiness of God by simply putting breath to four little words: "holy is his name" (v. 49b). For Mary to trust in an uncertain future, she had to look back at the certainty of a holy God. As Mary sang of the holiness of God, her song resonated with David's song found in Psalm 111:9 that reads: "He provided redemption for his people; he ordained his covenant forever—holy and awesome is his name." For Mary, she was looking back and remembering the unchanging nature of God. The God who was faithful and holy *then*, is still faithful and holy *now*.

Last, she sang of the mercy of God by declaring: "His mercy extends to those who fear him, from generation to generation" (v. 50).

Again, perhaps Mary took a cue from the Psalms and made it her own. The psalmist David wrote:

> The LORD is compassionate and gracious,
>   slow to anger, abounding in love.
> He will not always accuse,
>   nor will he harbor his anger forever;
> he does not treat us as our sins deserve
>   or repay us according to our iniquities.
> For as high as the heavens are above the earth,
>   so great is his love for those who fear him;

> as far as the east is from the west,
>> so far has he removed our transgressions from us.
>
> As a father has compassion on his children,
>> so the Lord has compassion on those who fear him[.] (103:8–13)

That, my friends, is mercy.

Someone said to me once, "Don't tell God how big your problems are. Tell your problems how big your God actually is."

Whatever stressors you have in your life today, take some notes from Mary. Remind those stressors about the mightiness of God, the holiness of God, and the mercy of God. Then look forward to what God has in store.

THE PRAYER

Almighty and Holy God, as we come before you today, we recognize your power and your righteousness. As we hold to your unfailing love, may we also surrender our future into your capable hands. Amen.

THE QUESTIONS

Today, let's look back. Where have you seen the mightiness of God in your life?

Where have you experienced the holiness of God in your life?

Where have you seen the mercy of God in your life?

14

DEEP DARKNESS AND A GREAT LIGHT

ISAIAH 9:2
The people walking in darkness
  have seen a great light;
on those living in the land of deep darkness
  a light has dawned.

CONSIDER THIS

One of my favorite times of the day during the season of Advent is early in the morning before the sun comes up, when the house is perfectly quiet and still. I'll fix a cup of coffee, grab my Bible, turn on our Christmas tree lights in the living room, and settle into my favorite chair. There's nothing quite like reading the Word by the light of the Christmas tree.

This morning, while reflecting over this devotional by twinkly lights, I must confess that I got curious. When *did* the first Christmas tree with electric lights happen and what was the story with that? Good news. There's a Wikipedia page for that.[10]

The year was 1882 and his name was Edward Johnson. Though you may not be familiar with his name, you might be more familiar with who he worked for: Thomas Edison. Edward Johnson was Edison's associate and served as the vice president of Edison Electric Light Company. On a cold day in December, he got a crazy idea to invent walnut-sized light bulbs in the colors of red, white, and blue, and string them on a Christmas tree that would illuminate and flicker when plugged in. Though it didn't catch on initially, the idea would eventually take root, and by 1930, most homes had them on their trees.

I can't help but think about how lights have changed over the years. My earliest memories of Christmas tree lights go back to my childhood and visits to my grandmother's house in East Texas. One of my favorite decorations at her house was an aluminum Christmas tree that had a color wheel that was plugged in next to it. Though that tree didn't have any lights on it, it was still magic. As the silver aluminum Christmas tree sat there, the color wheel would slowly turn, changing the tree into the colors of orange to green to red to blue. I would literally sit and stare at it, mesmerized. But, by

---

10. https://en.wikipedia.org/wiki/Christmas_lights.

far, my favorite Christmas lights were the ones on the other artificial tree at Grandmother's house; they were known as bubble lights. They literally got so warm that the liquid inside them would bubble in the spirit of old-school lava lamps.

Though the lights may have changed over the years, their purpose has not: to bring light into the darkness. No matter the setting or surroundings, no matter how dark a room or neighborhood street may be, once you flip on those small Christmas lights, the room or street takes on a different perspective. Illumination minimizes the darkness, and the world is just a little less scary as a result.

That's the beauty of light, and that was the promise and prophecy Isaiah made seven hundred years before that first Christmas morning.

In Isaiah 9 the Israelites had done it again. Though they were once in captivity in Egypt, God had led them into a place of freedom and the promised land. Yet, little by little, they wandered. The line from the hymn "Come, Thou Fount of Every Blessing" comes to mind: "Prone to wander, Lord, I feel it, prone to leave the God I love."[11] And that is exactly what happened to the Israelites.

---

11. Robert Robinson, "Come, Thou Fount of Every Blessing," 1758, public domain.

They wandered and, as a result, once again they found themselves in captivity—this time in Babylon.

It had to have been a dark and scary time for God's people. Yet it was here, within captivity and darkness, that Isaiah would throw out a spark of light and hope: "The people walking in darkness have seen a great light; on those living in the land of deep darkness a light has dawned" (9:2). How beautiful is this promise? Isaiah was declaring that a time was approaching that, not just darkness, but *deep* darkness would soon be illuminated by light, and that light was not just any ordinary light, it would be a *great* light.

Deep darkness cannot stand against the Great Light that is to come.

What was true seven hundred years before Christ's birth is just as relevant for us today, some two thousand years after his birth.

Perhaps a good suggestion for today is this: plug in this truth and shine that over the dark places of your life today.

THE PRAYER

God of wonder, we thank you for light. What comfort it brings us all to know that darkness does not and will not have the final word over our lives. Jesus, thank you for being the Light of the World. May we not only hold this light in our lives, but shine that light to all we encounter in Jesus's mighty name. Amen.

THE QUESTIONS

How does the imagery of light and darkness in the passage reflect the contrast between hope and despair we experience in our lives?

How can seeing this contrast impact the way we view the light of Christ at work in our lives today?

15
THE WONDER IN THE SEARCHING

MATTHEW 1:22–23
All this took place to fulfill what the Lord had said through the prophet: "The virgin will conceive and give birth to a son, and they will call him Immanuel" (which means "God with us").

In the summer of 1977, NASA launched two different spacecrafts from Cape Canaveral, Florida, named *Voyager 1* and *Voyager 2*. Their primary mission was to take pictures of Jupiter and Saturn, which they did successfully. But the mission didn't stop there. They just kept going, sending back data. In August of 2012, the first of both ships made history. *Voyager 1* made the historic entry into interstellar space, the region between stars filled with material discarded by the death of nearby stars believed to have happened millions of years ago. Three months later, *Voyager 2* crossed that milestone as well.

Ever since I was a little boy, things of space and spaceships have fascinated me. So I have followed these spacecrafts' travels for as long as I can remember. I loved seeing the images that were sent back and learning about the updates from the spacecrafts. However, what they have sent back was only part of the mission. They were also sent into space with a message.

Attached to both spacecrafts was a golden record.[12] On each record were a variety of natural sounds, such as the wind, waves, and various animal sounds like those of birds and whales in the ocean. Also attached were spoken greetings in more than fifty-five ancient and modern languages. There were also samplings of music. What's a golden record without music, right? The music that was added to the records consisted of everything from Bach to Mozart, Beethoven to Stravinsky, and my personal favorite, the addition of Chuck Berry's "Johnny B. Goode."[13]

I love the intentionality of the golden record, saying, "This is who we are," and sending that into outer space. However, the beauty of Advent is the reminder that what we've been searching for has already made contact

---

12. "What are the contents of the Golden Record?" NASA, https://voyager.jpl.nasa.gov/golden-record/whats-on-the-record/.

13. I can't help but imagine the day when intelligent life might send back a message that simply reads the following: "Send more Chuck Berry."

THE WONDER IN THE SEARCHING   67

with us—that which is beyond what we can see stepped into our world and literally came to us.

Reflect on that truth for just a moment. This is the story of the God of wonder, the Creator of the universe, the very one who breathed the stars into existence, stepping into our story, making contact with us to say, "Not only do I see you, but I am also becoming *one of you*."

It's a divine search-and-rescue mission that meets us all. When you learn this truth, you realize it changes everything. That which was lost has been found.

This leads us to our next story found in Matthew's gospel.

When I preach from the Gospels, I like to remind people that each gospel written is not just a book of the Bible, but it's a person's story—a personal narrative written from someone's perspective on what they have seen, heard, and learned about Jesus, God in flesh.

Matthew's perspective is written from someone who was a tax collector, overlooked and often despised by the Pharisees and Sadducees and often lumped in with prostitutes, lepers, and sinners. Yet Matthew was also the one who encountered Jesus and, from the Savior's lips, heard two words that would impact him and his story forever: "Follow me" (Matt. 9:9).

Perhaps this is why the gospel of Matthew begins and ends with a common theme. In Matthew 1, he records the angel's words to Joseph that Mary would have a son and he was to be named Immanuel, which means "God *with us*" (vv. 20–23, emphasis mine). Then in Matthew 28:20, the last words we see from Jesus are: "I am *with you* always, to the very end of the age" (emphasis mine).

The good news for us today is to sit with this truth: God is not a God who plays hide-and-seek with his creation. The season of Advent serves as a reminder for us all that no matter how lost or on the outside we may feel, not only have we already been found, he's with us this very moment.

THE PRAYER

Loving Father, what a gift your presence is in our lives. Today, may we keep open hands, inviting your Holy Spirit to guide us in the ways we should go. Thank you for your presence and provision. In Jesus's name we pray, amen.

THE QUESTIONS

Does God seem near or far to you in your story? How does Matthew's story mirror your own today?

16
LIGHT WILL GUIDE YOU HOME

MATTHEW 2:1–2

After Jesus was born in Bethlehem in Judea, during the time of King Herod, Magi from the east came to Jerusalem and asked, "Where is the one who has been born king of the Jews? We saw his star when it rose and have come to worship him."

CONSIDER THIS

In our journey through the nativity, let's take a few days in Matthew's gospel to look at some historical figures that take their place inside our nativity, even though they were actually late to the party. Let's talk about the wise men.

Here is an interesting fact. Matthew spends more time talking about the wise men and their pursuit of Jesus than he does on Mary and Joseph's story. Why do you think that is? Perhaps Matthew doesn't want us missing the story of the star and the seekers because maybe, just maybe, their story was Matthew's story. (Spoiler alert: it is our story as well.) Let's talk about the Magi, which some translations render as "wise men."

There is a lot we don't know about the Magi, but a few things we can assume from the opening verses found in the second chapter of Matthew: (1) they were astrologers who studied the stars, (2) they were also philosophers who may have had access to Jewish Scriptures, and (3) quite possibly the biggest thing to note, they were Gentiles, not actually a part of the Jewish faith. Why is this important? Because, as Gentiles, these Magi were *outside* of God's greater story.

Just imagine. On one ordinary average night, the Magi gather to talk stars and philosophy when a new star appears in the sky that was not to be found in their charts and maps. This star led them to God's Word and, perhaps, the prophecy of Daniel found in the Old Testament that spoke of the coming Messiah who would be hailed as the one who would come in the name of the Lord and be killed (9:24–26). Perhaps they also knew of Balaam's oracle found in Numbers 24, where he declared: "A star will come out of Jacob; a scepter will rise out of Israel" (v. 17b). We have no way of knowing for sure what Scriptures they had read. However, what we can know for certain is this: the star illuminated the way, God guided them, and they joyfully followed God's direction.

That is the power of light; it helps us find our way in the darkness.

In 1954, a navy pilot set out on a night training mission from an aircraft carrier off the coast of Japan.

As he lifted off in stormy weather, his directional finder inside the aircraft malfunctioned, and he unknowingly headed off in the wrong direction. If that's not bad enough, his instrument panel that was normally illuminated had also short-circuited, causing all his interior lights in the cockpit to go out and leaving him utterly and completely in the dark.

As the pilot looked around, all he saw was darkness. It was as if all that was outside his plane was now inside. That's a terrifying thought, isn't it? However, all was not lost. As he looked down on the dark waters of the ocean below him, his eye caught a mysterious glow. What the pilot saw was a faint blue-green glow trailing along the ocean's surface. Thankfully, he had trained and prepared enough to know that what he was looking at was a cloud of phosphorescent algae glowing in the sea. The pilot also knew that these particular algae would only glow when ships would stir it up as they traveled across the waters. The algae was showing the way.

According to the pilot, it was the "least reliable and most desperate method" of navigating a plane back to safety, but for future *Apollo 13* astronaut Jim Lovell, he knew it was *exactly* what he needed to do.[14] He simply

---

14. Rebecca Maksel, "Jim Lovell, from Carriers to the Moon," *Smithsonian Magazine*, April 2016, https://www.smithsonianmag.com/air-space-magazine/in-the-museum-space-capsules-180958440/.

followed the glowing phosphorescent algae as if it were a giant flashing arrow showing him the way back home.

Like Lovell, the Magi found themselves in a dark world. They had all this knowledge of stars and the Scriptures, yet they were not quite sure of their place in the middle of it all. But here is the beautiful truth: the wise men acted upon what they knew to be true. When they saw the star, when that flicker of light signaling the Light of the World had come into their story, that was all they needed. Their knowledge turned into action. Why? Jesus's story was worthy of their sacrifice, journey, and travel to come and worship him.

THE PRAYER

God of wonder, God of light, just as the Magi followed the star that led them to Jesus, so, too, we embark on a journey of faith, seeking out your presence and guidance. Today, we thank you for intertwining their story with ours, reminding us all of your faithfulness and the hope that comes from following your voice and call. Amen.

THE QUESTIONS

How does the light of Christ lead us today? What guides you and your story?

17
HEROD THE (NOT SO) GREAT

MATTHEW 2:3–8
When King Herod heard this he was disturbed, and all Jerusalem with him. When he had called together all the people's chief priests and teachers of the law, he asked them where the Messiah was to be born. "In Bethlehem in Judea," they replied, "for this is what the prophet has written:

*"'But you, Bethlehem, in the land of Judah,
  are by no means least among the rulers of Judah;
for out of you will come a ruler
  who will shepherd my people Israel.'"*

Then Herod called the Magi secretly and found out from them the exact time the star had appeared. He sent them to Bethlehem and said, "Go and search carefully for the child. As soon as you find him, report to me, so that I too may go and worship him."

CONSIDER THIS

When you take a little time to look at the facts and figures of "Herod the Great" in Jesus's day, you could say that he accomplished much during his administration. In the forty years he served as king of Judea before Christ's birth, he had kept the order and was responsible for many of the major building campaigns of the day, including the rebuilding of the temple of Jerusalem, designing and constructing several aqueducts in the region, as well as building the massive fortress known as Herodium, a.k.a. the "Mountain of the Little Paradise."

Of course, nothing gets built without the funds and money coming from somewhere. Where did it all come from? It came from the people of King Herod's day. The people certainly paid for all that expansion because Herod taxed them severely, so much that they could barely afford food for themselves, and starvation resulted. And that's when Herod would provide food for the people. In short, he had an uncanny ability of oppressing and stealing from the people, yet manipulating the outcome by making the people feel grateful for any food he gave them in return. It was a vicious and manipulative cycle.

So, on the outside, you could certainly say things were secure under Herod's reign. Buildings were built and his administration looked sound, yet under the hood, Herod the Great was not so great at all. Herod had a problem: power. Under all the accomplishments and what he was building externally, on the inside he was a tyrant, power-hungry, and threatened by anyone who could be perceived as greater, smarter, or more powerful than he was. To Herod, everyone was a suspect, including his own sons, whom he had killed for fear of them overthrowing him.

Knowing all of this now, re-read the Scripture for today's devotional and add those layers to Matthew's Christmas story.

Imagine the moment when these Magi from the East ride into Jerusalem with joy and praise and inquiring about the one true King—the Messiah born "King of the Jews"—the very same title that Herod had claimed for himself. This single event in Matthew's story has paranoia and disaster written all over it. Herod, addicted to power, learns this *other* king has come into the story—*his* story—and is faced with someone who could both challenge his authority and overthrow his rule. No wonder Herod is "disturbed," as Matthew so eloquently puts it (Matt. 2:3). Rest assured that when he gives the Magi a wink and smile and says, "Be sure you let me know when you find him so I can 'go and worship him' too" (v. 8), that was *not* Herod's intention.

Why are we spending time with King Herod today, and what is this story's place in our Christmas story? I think a good takeaway for us from today's text is this: it is never a bad thing to do a heart check. Whether we realize it or not, all of us can have a small dose of what I would call the "hidden Herod" inside of us.

At the core of Herod the Great was a fear of being insignificant and of being forgotten. Those feelings led him to push harder into power, which led to oppression, which resulted in murder. No matter how you look at it, the more you pursue power, the more you pursue control in your life, the harder you grip onto those things, the more you lose that which really matters. Because, guess what? It's not about you. When you realize the length God has gone to reach you through the gift of Jesus, it's more about what he desires to do within you and through you that matters most.

In this story today, let's acknowledge the darkness. It was a broken world then; it's still a broken world today. Yet there is hope in this story. Christ came into a dark world two thousand years ago, and that brings hope and light into our world today. That is good news for us all!

THE PRAYER

Almighty God, reveal to us the hidden Herods we might have tucked away in the secret places of our hearts. Help us loosen the grip of all control so that, with open hands, we can receive the love and acceptance you make available to each of us today. Amen.

THE QUESTIONS

Herod had a great deal of darkness that he kept hidden. What's the danger in that?

Where is control, power, and a fear of insignificance hiding in the hidden places of your heart? How does this story free us from those things?

18
GPS: GOD'S POSITIONING SYSTEM

MATTHEW 2:9–12
After they had heard the king, they went on their way, and the star they had seen when it rose went ahead of them until it stopped over the place where the child was. When they saw the star, they were overjoyed. On coming to the house, they saw the child with his mother Mary, and they bowed down and worshiped him. Then they opened their treasures and presented him with gifts of gold, frankincense and myrrh. And having been warned in a dream not to go back to Herod, they returned to their country by another route.

CONSIDER THIS

Does anyone else find it somewhat strange that most of us, when we're in our car and traveling to unknown destinations, don't really know how to get where we're going? We simply put the address in whatever navigational system we are using, put the car in drive, and head out on the open road. Usually, these maps do their job. They recognize shortcuts, know when there are hazards ahead, and even alert us to delays that are in our path. I love it when these maps work; not so much when they don't.

Recently, my wife and I were going to attend the wedding of some family friends and flew into an airport and rented a car. Not knowing exactly where the venue was but having the address, we put the venue location into the map app and away we went. About two hours into the trip, we pulled over to grab some lunch, and that's when it happened—after we put the car in park, the normally calm voice on the GPS system somehow lost our location. So, much to our surprise, it just began giving a myriad of instructions.

"Turn right." "Turn left." "Turn left." "Turn right." "Turn right." "Turn right." Honest to goodness, it was a nonstop tirade of commands with limited breaths in between.

My wife and I just looked at each other and laughed until we cried. I'm not sure how the GPS system lost our location, nor do I know why it flipped out and started throwing every direction that was loaded into its directional database at us, but it was clearly going to do whatever it had to do to get us back on the path we were supposed to go.

You know, God has a pretty good track record of doing the same.

Go back to the exodus story. How did God lead his people? "By day the Lord went ahead of them in a pillar of cloud to guide them on their way and by night in a pillar of fire to give them light, so that they could travel by day or night" (13:21). I love that, during the day, it was a cloud, but at night—when traveling in uncertain places can be the scariest, when you can't see what's waiting around every corner—it was light that guided the steps of his people. It's here, within the story of the Magi, that God would do it again.

Having left Herod and knowing the direction they were to head (Bethlehem, but not knowing the address), God would send a star—literally, a light—to lead the way. It would not just lead the way; it would stop over the house where Jesus was.

Can you imagine? No wonder "they were overjoyed" (Matt. 2:10). What happened next is so beautiful: "On coming to the house, they saw the child with his mother Mary, and they bowed down and worshiped him" (v. 11a). They literally fell on their faces before the Lord.

Did you know in the Gospels there are thirteen instances of a person or persons taking a position of bowing, falling on their faces at the feet of Jesus? The very first instance is right here—a group of Gentiles who traveled at great cost and expense arrived at their destination, and with childlike wonder, their knees buckled and they fell on their faces in worship and adoration before Jesus.

Then there were the gifts. Gold is a gift you would give a king. Frankincense is an incense often used for worship in the temple; it could be considered a priestly gift. Myrrh is a perfume often used to anoint dead bodies placed in a tomb. I suppose there is a reason they were called "wise" men.

What follows the story is a lot of "we don't know." They received a dream to stay away from Herod, so that's exactly what they did. They returned to their home via a different route, but I strongly suspect they did not return home as they left it. They returned changed because they had encountered wonder after wonder in their pursuit of Jesus.

Their journey was not a wasted one; it led them to the King of kings.

Your journey is not wasted, my friend. May that same wonder find you today, wherever you are in your story.

THE PRAYER

God of wonder, just as a GPS guides our earthly journey, we thank you for being our Divine Navigator, leading us on the path of righteousness. With gratitude, we trust in your leading, God, knowing that your way is the right way. May we follow as you lead. Amen.

THE QUESTIONS

Can you think of a time in your life that your journey led to something beautiful and unexpected?

How did you find Jesus? Reflect on that experience. What did it mean then and what does it mean to you today?

19

THE WONDER IN THE WORKING

LUKE 2:8
And there were shepherds living out in the fields nearby, keeping watch over their flocks at night.

CONSIDER THIS

As I write this, there's a short viral video that's making the rounds on the Internet that, honestly, has the makings of *childlike wonder* written all over it.

The video shows six-year-old little Milo from the UK sitting in the back seat of his mother's car. Apparently, he has just gotten out of school and couldn't wait to share with her the part that he had been given in the school's nativity play.

"Guess what I am for the nativity?" Milo exclaims, "I'm a classic one!"

His mother pauses for a moment and then responds, "Joseph?"

"No," says Milo.

"One of the wise men?" his mother replies.

Again, Milo shakes his head and gives a, "No," with a smile.

Milo's mother, fresh out of guesses, says, "You're just going to have to tell me then."

And that's when Milo's face lights up and he says, "I'm Door Holder Number Three. I'll be holding doors!" Incredible. I'm certain the video is viral because that's *not* the answer you would have expected. But wait, it gets better—the next part is my absolute favorite. When Milo's mother asked him what he did when he found out about the role, he simply said to himself, "I'm a door holder. Get in there . . . let's go! *Yes!*"[15]

Milo may not have gotten the part he might have expected, but if he did want another role, you'd never know it. He was just thrilled to play a *part*, and even as Door Holder Number Three, he was going to get in there and hold that door like no one had ever held a door before.

I wonder: Would our lives would look differently if we approached this day with that kind of childlike wonder? I love the way Eugene Peterson translates what the apostle Paul said in Romans 12:1–2 taken from the Message translation. "So, here's what I want you to do,

---

15. https://www.tiktok.com/@itsgoneviral/video/7306534433144769825?lang=en.

God helping you: Take your everyday, ordinary life—your sleeping, eating, going-to-work, and walking-around life—and place it before God as an offering. Embracing what God does for you is the best thing you can do for him." Paul, to the early church, was simply saying that we should keep open eyes and open hands to what God may be doing in and through us every single day. What a reminder to know that worship is not just something we attend; it's a lifestyle.

Today we move back into Luke's gospel, and we take a closer look at some other people found in our nativity scene that perhaps didn't see themselves as key players in God's greater story: the shepherds.

To understand the shepherds of Jesus's day, it helps to see them from a first-century perspective. Shepherds were the bottom of the social ladder. They were mostly uneducated and oftentimes considered as dishonest, unreliable, and unsavory characters—at least, that was the perception of the religious leaders of the day. One more occupational hazard that came with the job of tending the sheep: they weren't allowed in the temple. Sheep required care seven days a week. So, unable to abide by the man-made Sabbath regulations, shepherds were considered by the religious leaders of the day to be ceremonially unclean; therefore, keeping them from ever entering into the temple.

Take that in for a moment.

They had a job. They did it dutifully. But, amidst it all, they were overlooked, unseen, and church had no place for them because of the nature of their dirty job.

Yet, the shepherds *were* seen, and to them, God would reveal the news of his Son coming into our world and story who would be for us all the Good Shepherd (John 10:11), and whose name would be the name above all names (Philippians 2:9).

That, my friends, is the good news of the gospel.

This is the God we worship.

Perhaps you feel unseen, overlooked, and stained from whatever sin that's still sticking to you, or maybe you have been given a label from the world. Hear this: you have value. You are not only seen by the Creator of the universe, but you are loved as well.

Today, let's get in there . . . let's go! *Yes!*

THE PRAYER

Gracious God, today we say, *thank you*. Just as you saw and used shepherds then, may we remember that you not only see us today, but you also value us, regardless of status or circumstances. May we hold to beauty found in this truth that intersects with our own lives today. Amen.

THE QUESTIONS

Do you have anything in common with the shepherds? Where's the hope found in this story for each of us today?

20
DROP THE BLANKET

LUKE 2:9–11
An angel of the Lord appeared to them, and the glory of the Lord shone around them, and they were terrified. But the angel said to them, "Do not be afraid. I bring you good news that will cause great joy for all the people. Today, in the town of David a Savior has been born to you; he is the Messiah, the Lord."

CONSIDER THIS

The year was 1965. Pull up the headlines of the day and you would find that the country was still reeling from John F. Kennedy's assassination. The Vietnam War was intensifying and the march in Selma, Alabama, was making national and world news. To say that things were strained in our country would be an understatement. It was a difficult and dark time, and that's exactly why a cartoonist named Charles Schultz thought the world needed a little hope. So on December 9, 1965, the world was introduced to the classic, *A Charlie Brown Christmas*.

If you've seen it, you'll remember that Charlie Brown was finding it difficult to find joy at Christmastime.

When tasked with putting on the Christmas play, Charlie Brown made it his goal to find the perfect Christmas tree to showcase on stage. Of course, the tree he ended up with was not ideal. It was small, pretty thinned out, and didn't look like the picture-perfect tree everyone had hoped for. But for Charlie, it was perfect. That was, until everyone else gave their opinions. Where Charlie saw beauty in the little tree, everyone else saw imperfection, and the disdain they had for that little tree they put on the shoulders of Charlie Brown, leading him to shout out the following question: "Isn't there anyone who knows what Christmas is all about?"

Linus had the answer. He quietly walked to center stage, his trademark blue security blanket in hand, and recited Luke's Christmas story in the good old King James. If ever there's a moment of childlike wonder, this was it.

I've seen *A Charlie Brown Christmas* a hundred times, but there's a little hidden gem found inside Linus's reading of the Christmas story that I had not noticed until recently. Perhaps you've missed it as well. When Linus got to Luke 2:9 and read the angel's proclamation, "Do not be afraid," Linus dropped his blue security blanket. It is important to note that you will never see Linus let go of his blanket in any of the comic strips. Not intentionally, at least. But here he did. Why? It's as if

Linus was saying to us all that security and comfort isn't always found in what we're holding on to; it's found in what's holding us—the good news of this Christmas story, Immanuel, Christ with us.

That's the gospel message.

But wait, Linus wasn't quite finished yet. He then took the scrawny tree that held such ridicule and shame, and he placed his blue security blanket around the base of it, showing us all that comfort and joy wraps itself around the misshaped and overlooked, the unwanted and the undesirable. Linus was preaching the gospel message, my friends.

Now, back to the shepherds. On a particularly dark and ordinary night, it was to a group of overlooked and undesirable shepherds working on a hillside that the good news of great joy for all people was given. That's radical wonder.

God could have given this news to royalty. He could have delivered it to a king or priest, but he started with shepherds. They were the first hearers, believers, and preachers of the Christmas gospel.

What are you holding on to a little too tightly today? Drop the blanket and let this story wrap itself around you. Find comfort in this truth today!

THE PRAYER

Eternal God, we thank you for the promise that is found for us all within words, "Do not be afraid." We ask today that whatever anxiety, worries, or fears we may be holding on to be released through your power, leaving our empty hands to take hold of the good news of great joy that is for all people. In Jesus's name, amen.

THE QUESTIONS

What might you be holding on to today? Perhaps a better question is this: What might the Lord be encouraging you to let go of?

21

BIG THINGS, LITTLE PACKAGE

ISAIAH 9:6
For to us a child is born,
  to us a son is given,
  and the government will be on his shoulders.
And he will be called
  Wonderful Counselor, Mighty God,
  Everlasting Father, Prince of Peace.

CONSIDER THIS

There's a story attributed to author and poet Robert Louis Stevenson, who was traveling once on a ship that found itself in a severe storm and in imminent danger of sinking. According to Stevenson, many of the passengers began to whisper to one another, "Are we going down? Are we safe?" After a few moments of conversation among the passengers, one brave soul volunteered to travel up to the pilot house and see the captain.

Bold move.

As the passenger made his way through the rain and wind and stepped in to see the captain, it's said that the

BIG THINGS, LITTLE PACKAGE 93

water-soaked passenger saw the pilot standing calmly with his hands firmly on the wheel. The passenger, filled with fear, witnessed the captain slowly turn and make eye contact with him and, without saying a word, simply smile. That was it. No words. Just a smile. Apparently, that was all that passenger needed to see.

As he traveled back down to the main cabin, the once-fearful passenger exclaimed, "We're going to be all right. I've seen the face of the captain and, good news: he smiled at me."

I think of that story often.

Truth be told, it's easy to run into turbulence in our world today. You don't have to look very far to see the news stories of conflict, heartache, or tragedy that seem to make their way into our daily headlines.

Yet here's a good question of wonder for us today: Where are we looking to find our hope and assurance amidst the uncertainties and storms we see raging in the world?

Let's go back to Isaiah 9. Remember, to a people in captivity, Isaiah reminded the Israelites of light that was on the horizon; the time of deep darkness was coming to an end, and with it, another promise: "For to us a child is born, to us a son is given, and the government will be on his shoulders. And he will be called Wonderful Counselor, Almighty God, Everlasting Father, Prince of Peace" (v. 6).

When Mary and Joseph looked down upon their sleeping baby in the straw-filled manger on that first Christmas night, did these words from Isaiah come to mind? How could all of these really big titles fit into such a small, tiny, and infant package?

Yet Jesus fulfilled every single one of them.

Jesus is our Wonderful Counselor. He's literally the wonder of God found in human form. Isaiah added that, "The Spirit of the Lord will rest on him—the Spirit of wisdom and of understanding, the Spirit of counsel and of might, the Spirit of the knowledge and fear of the Lord—" (11:2). Good news: he doesn't hold office hours. His counsel is available to all who ask, and the wood of that nativity would eventually be exchanged for the wood of the cross and, on it, he paid the price for us all. He is our Wonderful Counselor.

Jesus is Almighty God. He's not just the wonder of God found in human form; he is literally Almighty. The same God who breathed the stars into existence and breath into Adam's nostrils is the same Jesus who calmed the wind and waves, told the demons where to go, and healed the broken and afflicted. Jesus declared: "I am the Alpha and the Omega who is, and who was, and who is to come, the Almighty" (Rev. 1:8). You may not have it all together, my friend. Good news: he is not just all together; he is also *All Mighty*.

Jesus is our Everlasting Father. In Luke 15, Jesus told a parable about a young man who does the unthinkable: he asks his father for his inheritance, which is the same thing as saying, "Hey Dad, can we just fast-forward to that part where you die and give me the money now?" It's a shocking and unthinkable thing to do, yet even more shocking was the fact that the father relents and gives his son the inheritance. Time passes and the son squanders it away, realizes the mistake he had made, and repents. It is a long walk home to face the music, but wait for it . . . what does the father do? He runs to meet his son and welcome him back home.

That's the picture of our Everlasting Father. It's not a temporary love. It's not a contractual love. It's an everlasting love that the Father has for you. No matter how far you wander from the Father, he will always be there to welcome you back home.

Jesus is our Prince of Peace. Just as a prince works to bring peace and unity to his kingdom, Jesus brings peace into the hearts of believers. To his disciples, he said, "Peace I leave with you; my peace I give you. I do not give to you as the world gives. Do not let your hearts be troubled and do not be afraid" (John 14:27). That is a peace that passes all understanding (Phil 4:7), and it is a gift ready to be unwrapped and claimed this very moment.

Perhaps you have a storm raging in your life. Take a moment and catch the eye of the one whose hands are firmly at the wheel, and then remind yourself of the following: "I'm going to be all right. I've seen the face of the captain and, good news: he smiled at me."

THE PRAYER

God of wonder, we thank you that, in Jesus, we have a Wonderful Counselor, the Almighty God, Everlasting Father, and Prince of Peace. Today may we rest in the knowledge that you hold everything perfectly in your hands. Amen.

THE QUESTIONS

Can you name a storm in your life where you've found comfort in knowing who was guiding the ship?

On a piece of paper, write down these four attributes of Jesus—Wonderful Counselor, Almighty God, Everlasting Father, Prince of Peace—at the top. From there, write down what each means to you and where you need Jesus to meet you within those names.

22
HERE'S YOUR SIGN

LUKE 2:12–15
"This will be a sign to you: You will find a baby wrapped in cloths and lying in a manger."

Suddenly a great company of the heavenly host appeared with the angel, praising God and saying,

"Glory to God in the highest heaven,
and on earth peace to those on whom his favor rests."

When the angels had left them and gone into heaven, the shepherds said to one another, "Let's go to Bethlehem and see this thing that has happened, which the Lord has told us about."

CONSIDER THIS

I love the seven words that kick off our text for today: "This will be a sign to you." Let's be honest. We all need a good flashing neon sign in our lives, don't we? That's one of the many things I love about this Christmas story. There are signs and wonders all over it.

Zechariah and Mary got an angel; not just any angel, they got the one with a name, Gabriel. The Magi got a star; not just any star, a moving star that led them to where they were supposed to go! Today, the shepherds get the same gift. The sign that they are looking for is a baby wrapped in swaddling clothes and lying in a manger.

We'll look at the significance of "swaddling cloths" found in the gospel text (Luke 2:12 ESV). Let's go back to the shepherds "living out in the fields nearby, keeping watch over their flocks at night" (v. 8). It's what you would assume shepherds would do, correct? But there's something special in relationship to these shepherds. Make no mistake, these were no ordinary shepherds. Sure, they did what ordinary shepherds would have done—watching over their flock, keeping them from harm, and helping to deliver the newborn lambs as they came into the world. So why were they special? Three words give us the clue: location, location, location.

The shepherds were watching their flock out in the fields near Bethlehem, which is about five miles from Jerusalem. Given the proximity to where these shepherds were located, these shepherds were most likely priestly shepherds, meaning they both cared for the flock as well as provided the sacrificial lambs for the temple in Jerusalem. For a lamb to be worthy of sacrifice in the temple, there were certain conditions that had to be met. The lamb had to be spotless and unblemished. The shepherds would do two things with the newborns: they would inspect the lambs born out in the field meticulously, making sure they were flawless and without fault, and they would wrap the lambs in swaddling clothes, certifying their birth was a "holy birth" deemed as an acceptable sacrifice.

Imagine the moment these shepherds heard the angels proclaim the Savior had come into the world, and he would be found wrapped in swaddling clothes and lying in a manger. To the shepherds, they would have understood the announcement in a way most of us might have missed. It was the announcement of a holy birth, a baby, the Messiah, unblemished and without fault, wrapped in swaddling clothes and lying in a manger.

When one angel announced the birth to the shepherds, it didn't take long for all of heaven to join them as they sang out their first Christmas carol, "Glory to God in the highest heaven, and on earth peace to those on whom his favor rests" (v. 14). Then, the lights went out. Moments before, the Bethlehem hillside was illuminated by the glory of the angels singing and praising together. In an instant, darkness fell back over the hillside.

I imagine the shepherds stood there momentarily, looking at one another and blinking their eyes. Then, suddenly in the stillness and the darkness of the night, one of the shepherds spoke up and said, "Perhaps we should go check this out."

And off they ran.

THE PRAYER

God of wonder, as the angels joined their voices together in the heavenly chorus, "Glory to God in the highest," may we join our voices and hearts in the same song today. Like the shepherds, may we move toward this same good news the angels pointed them to. Amen.

THE QUESTIONS

Looking at the text again for today, what was the response of the angels to the good news of great joy for all people, and what was the response of the shepherds?

What would our world be like had they kept quiet?

What should our response be today?

23
WORTH THE WAIT

MICAH 5:2
"But you, Bethlehem Ephrathah,
  though you are small among the clans of Judah,
out of you will come for me
  one who will be ruler over Israel,
whose origins are from old,
  from ancient times."

CONSIDER THIS

His name was Phillips Brooks.

Brooks was a pastor of a small community church and he had hit a wall. Exhausted and spent emotionally and mentally from the day-to-day operations, sadly, he found himself in a familiar place that many in ministry can easily come to—a place of burnout. He just didn't have much left in the tank to give. So he went to the leadership of his church and asked for some time off and inquired about the possibility of taking an extended sabbatical. The leadership of his church approved, and when Brooks was asked where he'd like to go, he threw out the idea of a dream, visiting the Holy Land. So he booked the trip and off he went on his adventure.

Now, I have been to the Holy Land several times, but somehow, Brooks was able to book something I have yet to do: he rode a horse from Jerusalem to Bethlehem on Christmas Eve. And, to make matters even sweeter, he arrived at the Church of the Nativity *just* in time for Christmas Eve services.

After the service had ended, which was said to have been five hours long, he walked out of the church at the midnight hour on Christmas Day and suddenly became completely overwhelmed by the beauty of the Christmas story. He had read and preached the Christmas story so many times before; however, on this particular night, the Christmas story read and preached the glory of the gospel to him. Brooks experienced a moment of awe and true wonder, caught off guard by the darkness of the little town contrasted by the brightness of the stars on that night, but, more than anything, how this Advent story had been *his* story.

Before traveling back to his church, he thought he would capture the moment by writing down some lyrics he hoped would become a song he could gift to his church. So he grabbed pen and paper and began to write down the following lyrics: "O little town of Bethlehem, how still we see thee lie; above thy deep and dreamless sleep the silent stars go by. Yet in thy dark streets shineth the everlasting Light; the hopes and fears of all the years are met in thee tonight."[16] The year was 1868 and, unbeknownst to Phillips Brooks, those scribbled-out lyrics would turn into the beloved Christmas hymn, "O Little Town of Bethlehem," which is still being sung today.

Long before Phillips Brooks wrote that, there was another verse written about that same little town of Bethlehem. It wasn't a song, however; it was a prophecy spoken by Micah regarding the hope that would come through that little city (Mic. 5:2) some seven hundred years before that first Christmas Day.

In Micah's day, God's people had a lot to fear. Israel was still in rebellion against God, and Micah didn't shy away from speaking about a coming judgment. It was harsh, involving Babylonian captivity and some really difficult years ahead. Yet amid the fears, amid the darkness still to come, there would also be a sliver of some much-needed hope. Through this little city, the Messiah would come.

The birth of Jesus in Bethlehem, a humble and unexpected setting, mirrored the fulfillment of Micah's prophecy and signified the perfect timing and faithfulness of God. Think about that. Israel got this news seven hundred years before the Messiah was to come! That's

---

16. Phillips Brooks, words; Lewis H. Redner, music, "O Little Town of Bethlehem," 1868, public domain.

a long time to wait. Yet it was worth the wait because God's timing will always be divine timing. As Paul said to the church of Galatia, "But when the fullness of time had come, God sent forth his Son" (Gal. 4:4a ESV). At just the right moment, through the birth of Jesus, we're reminded that the good news of God's plan and redemption has come into our story.

Let this story preach to you today. Just as Micah's words were fulfilled in Jesus, may we find comfort and joy as we are reminded that God's promises are true, his words are trustworthy, and, within this Christmas story, we can all be reminded: "the hopes and fears of all the years are met in thee tonight."[17]

THE PRAYER

Heavenly Father, what a joy it is to remember that this is not just a story to be told; it is also a story to be received. Breathe the wonder of this good news into our lives and hearts today and may we exhale with joy the story to all we encounter. In Jesus's mighty name, amen.

---

17. Brooks and Redner, "O Little Town of Bethlehem."

THE QUESTIONS

Find the lyrics to "O Little Town of Bethlehem" and read them as a prayer.

What lines in the song register with you? What hopes and fears do you hold that could be met in Christ today?

24

HEARERS, BELIEVERS, AND PREACHERS

LUKE 2:16–18

So they hurried off and found Mary and Joseph, and the baby, who was lying in the manger. When they had seen him, they spread the word concerning what had been told them about this child, and all who heard it were amazed at what the shepherds said to them.

CONSIDER THIS

Of all the jobs the shepherds had in their daily to-do list, one was of utmost importance: to take care of and provide for the sheep. However, when news comes to them that Jesus was in their midst—the Messiah, the Savior of the world, had come into their world—what they *thought* was primary became secondary. Why? Because when Jesus is in your midst, you quickly discover that he is the most necessary and important thing.

What did the shepherds do? Luke records that they "hurried off" (Luke 2:16).

Notice what they *didn't* do. They didn't brush aside the angelic encounter as a reaction to some bad hummus they had the night before. They didn't huddle up together and discuss the pros and cons of whether they should heed the angel's directions. They didn't pause, ponder, and then reply, "Perhaps we should pray for further direction?"

They heard the good news and acted on it.

In Matthew's gospel, Jesus told the story of a shepherd who would leave ninety-nine sheep to go after the stray one (18:12–13). How beautiful that, here, the shepherds left their flock to go after one single lamb, the Lamb of God.

They find themselves in the presence of Mary, Joseph, and Jesus, wondering and marveling in awe. And then they left and spread the exciting word, "glorifying and praising God for all the things they had heard and seen, which were just as they had been told" (Luke 2:20). The shepherds were the first hearers, the first believers, and the first preachers of the Christmas gospel.

God broke the wall between heaven and earth, delivering the good news, and that good news went straight to their hearts. They not only heard the message, but they also *received* the message. The Christmas gospel went from head to heart, and then heart to feet, as they went to experience it for themselves. Isn't that the beauty that awaits us all on this Christmas Eve?

It's one thing to hear about Jesus and peek inside the manger this evening and think to ourselves, "What a lovely and beautiful story." Yet the truth is, this story doesn't just call us to look back at the birth of Christ, it moves us to discover that Jesus desires to be born within each of us. We can attend Christmas Eve services for every single year we're alive, yet if Christ is never born in our hearts, we've missed the story completely.

Jesus, who was born in the world, desires to find his way into your heart. That's the beauty that finds us on Christmas Eve.

THE PRAYER

Heavenly Father, on this Christmas Eve, may we gather in awe of the childlike wonder found in the story of Jesus's birth. May we embrace the joy and the innocence of that holy night, and may it ignite our faith, warm our hearts, and bring hope unto us all. Amen.

THE QUESTIONS

What did the shepherds do after they found the baby in the manger, and what example does this set for those who find Jesus today?

Where does this story encourage you, and where does this story challenge you within your own context today?

25
IT IS GOD'S DARK

JOHN 1:1–5

In the beginning was the Word, and the Word was with God, and the Word was God. He was with God in the beginning. Through him all things were made; without him nothing was made that has been made. In him was life, and that life was the light of all mankind. The light shines in the darkness, and the darkness has not overcome it.

CONSIDER THIS

It started in November with a single string of Christmas lights on a Baltimore County street. Kim Morton was watching a holiday movie with her daughter when she received a text from her neighbor that encouraged her to look outside.

When she looked out her front door, she was surprised to see that her neighbor across the street, Matt, had taken a string of white Christmas lights and hung them from his house, over the street, connecting them to a tree in her yard. She looked down to see that he had also left a tin of homemade cookies on her porch.

So why the gesture?

Matt knew that his neighbor was facing a dark time. When she moved into the neighborhood, Matt and his family got to know Kim and learned a little of her story. She had recently been dealing with a lot of anxiety and some depression, as well as grieving the loss of a loved one while also carrying stress at work. So, in Matt's words, "I was simply hoping to brighten her world and let her know that she was not alone."[18]

Here's where the story takes an unexpected turn.

The neighbors began to talk, mostly out of curiosity as to why Matt had connected a string of Christmas lights from his house to Kim's house. What transpired over the next several days caught everyone on the street by surprise.

One by one, the neighbors began stringing Christmas lights from their house to the neighbor's house across the street. Less than seven days later, the entire neighborhood had taken that one small gesture of love and carried it forward, spreading light up and down this quiet little suburban neighborhood.[19]

---

18. Sydney Page, "A Man Strung Christmas Lights from His Home to His Neighbor's to Support Her. The Whole Community Followed," *Washington Post*, December 21, 2021, https://www.washingtonpost.com/lifestyle/2021/12/21/baltimore-rodgers-forge-christmas-lights/.
19. Ibid.

IT IS GOD'S DARK

I love this story because of its organic nature. There was nothing planned or organized. It was simply one neighbor reminding another neighbor that they were not alone, and that one small gesture sparked a movement that others wanted to be a part of.

Isn't this the Christmas story? Today we are reminded that light has come into our world.

If there's anyone who loves to tell the story of light and Jesus, it's the gospel writer John. With more than thirty references to light in his gospel, the first you find here: "In him was life, and that life was the light of all mankind" (John 1:4). What follows that truth? "The light shines in the darkness, and the darkness has not overcome it" (v. 5).

To know this story of Christmas is to know that darkness need not be a worry any longer because light has come.

I heard a story recently of a little boy who always slept with a night-light in his room because he was afraid of the dark. Then one Christmas Eve, the pastor read this passage from John 1 and the young boy took it to heart. After the service, he asked his mom if Jesus *really* is "the light [that] shines in the darkness" (v. 5).

She smiled and said, "Why, yes. He certainly is!" He didn't say anything, and the mother thought nothing else of it.

When it came time for bed, she tucked him in, kissed him on the forehead, and went to turn on the night-light. As she did, her little boy stopped her and confidently declared, "Don't worry about the night-light, Mom. I don't need it any longer."

Shocked, the mom replied, "I thought you were afraid of the dark?"

Her son looked at her and replied, "It is God's dark, Mom. I don't need it."

Isn't that a truth we all need to remember?

Today we celebrate the good news that light has come, but may we also remember that the light of Christ needs to be shared. So let's be extravagant in the way we take the good news of Jesus and stretch that light out to all we encounter. The world will be brighter because of it.

THE PRAYER

God of wonder, on this blessed Christmas Day, we pray the radiant light of Christ's love would shine upon us all, guiding our hearts and filling our very lives with joy and peace. Father, help us to not only receive the light of Christ, but to be reflectors of his light and love—on this Christmas Day, and each day to come. In the name of Jesus, amen.

THE QUESTIONS

Though the Advent journey has ended, how can you take this story and carry it with you into the New Year? The Christmas decorations will soon be put away, but may I give a suggestion? Leave a nativity set up year-round, reminding you of this story that should never be put away! Let it serve as a 365-day reminder of the good news of great joy that is for us all!